# WOULD YOU RATHER

## Game Book For Kids
## Ages 6 - 12

Fun, Silly, Thought-Provoking & Witty Questions

With
Illustrations
&
Bonus

© Copyright 2024 by Phoe Sprints
All rights reserved.

It is illegal to reproduce, duplicate, or transmit any part of this book in either electronic or in print. This extends to creating a secondary or tertiary copy of the work or a recorded copy and is only allowed with express written consent from the Publisher.

All additional rights reserved.

# Table of Contents

1. Introduction                                    1
2. Rules of the Game                               5
3. Would You Rather...                             6
4. Gross Edition                                  80
5. Bonus                                          86

# INTRODUCTION

We would like to personally **thank you** for purchasing this book.

I have no special talents. I am only passionately curious.
#### - Albert Einstein

Curiosity gives children the confidence to try new things. The more a child explores, the more he/she learns.

Learning starts with us. As parents, teachers, caretakers, relatives, or well-wishers, we should encourage children to stay curious, read more, learn and grow. This is exactly what we had in mind while creating this "Would You Rather" book.

We hope you will have as much fun exploring these questions as we did in making them.

# RULES OF THE GAME

The rules of the game are simple, and you can play it with your friends and family. The more, the merrier!

**If you have two players**
1. One player starts by asking a "Would you rather" question, followed by "Why?"
2. The next player chooses an option and explains why they picked that one. The explanations can be silly, logical, hilarious, well-thought-out, or creative! These explanations often lead to funny and interesting conversations!
3. Pass the book to the next person, and they get to ask their "Would you rather" question.

**If you have more players**
1. Keep going around the circle until everyone gets their turn to ask a question and give their answer.

**Alternatively:**
1. Decide who will be the Question Master. This person will ask one question from the book each round.
2. The other players take turns answering the question.
3. The game ends when everyone has had a turn. The Question Master can choose the winner who gave the best answer.

## Now let's get creative!!

# WOULD YOU RATHER...

Hop everywhere like a bunny
or
Crawl like a crab for a day?

Sit on nails
or
sit on ice?

# WOULD YOU RATHER...

Step through quicksand
or
jump over lava?

See the Northern lights
or
a jumping whale?

# WOULD YOU RATHER...

See a bear or a skunk outside your tent while camping?

Bring a bug spray
or
Sunscreen to the camping?

# WOULD YOU RATHER...

Drink coke with milk
or
yogurt?

Be the funniest person alive
or
the smartest person alive?

# WOULD YOU RATHER...

Be able to visit mars
or
the moon?

Travel to Antarctica and see penguins
or
to Africa and see lions?

# WOULD YOU RATHER...

Eat pizza
or
ice cream as your only meal for the rest of your life?

Get stung by a jellyfish
or
get pinched by a crab?

# WOULD YOU RATHER...

Be a giant mouse
or
a tiny elephant?

Replace your toothpaste
with hot sauce
or
replace your shampoo with salsa?

# WOULD YOU RATHER...

Dress like a clown
or
an astronaut for a week?

Surf in the ocean with
a bunch of sharks
or
surf with a bunch of jellyfish?

Eat something spicy
or
bitter for the rest of your life?

# WOULD YOU RATHER...

Win a million dollars
or
be able to read people's minds?

Have super bushy eyebrows
or
no eyebrows at all?

Be smarter than the smartest
or
stronger than the strongest?

## WOULD YOU RATHER...

Keep flamingos as pets
or
peacocks?

Spend a day living as a dolphin underwater
or
swinging through trees like a monkey in the jungle?

Have tiger's stripes
or
porcupine's needles?

# WOULD YOU RATHER...

Have the power to manipulate electricity or gravity?

Farm vegetables

or

raise cattle for a living?

# WOULD YOU RATHER...

Have the ability to
time travel to the past
or
the future?

Have a career as
a famous musician
or
as a respected scientist?

# WOULD YOU RATHER...

Have a neighbor who talks to garden gnomes
or
hosts alien-themed parties?

Have a friend who always wears
mismatched socks
or
one who speaks in movie quotes?

# WOULD YOU RATHER...

Ride a helicopter
or
a parachute to school?

Have an extra ear
or
an extra nose?

# WOULD YOU RATHER...

Every holiday be Christmas
or
every holiday be Halloween?

wear a swimsuit in the snow
or
a big coat on the hottest day
of summer?

# WOULD YOU RATHER...

Constantly itch
or
always have to sneeze?

Wear a new shirt inside out every day
or
mismatched new shoes everyday?

# WOULD YOU RATHER...

Have a pet kangaroo from Australia
or
a panda from China?

Be a character in a funny film
or
in an action-adventure?

# WOULD YOU RATHER...

Be invisible
or
be able to fly?

Be ten years older
or
four years younger?

# WOULD YOU RATHER...

Have a hand twice as big
or
half as small?

Chased by a stampede of giggling unicorns
or
a mob of penguins wearing party hats?

# WOULD YOU RATHER...

Camp in your backyard
or
have a picnic in the park?

Shrink down to the size of an ant
or
grow as tall as a skyscraper?

# WOULD YOU RATHER...

Be only able to whisper
or
only able to shout?

Have teeth that glow in the dark
or
hair that glows in the dark?

# WOULD YOU RATHER...

Be an evil wizard in a fairy tale
or
a character no one remembers?

Build a secret fort
in the woods
or
a sandcastle
at the beach?

# WOULD YOU RATHER...

Have a travel buddy who tells funny jokes
but never stops talking
or one who falls asleep and snores loudly?

Have a wallet that spits confetti whenever
you use it to pay
or a piggy bank that oinks whenever you
save money?

# WOULD YOU RATHER...

Camp on the beach
or
in the mountains?

Use a microscope
or
a magnifying glass?

Have feathers
or fur?

# WOULD YOU RATHER...

Live on a farm surrounded by nature
or in a bustling city filled
with skyscrapers and people?

Live on the moon
or
a space station?

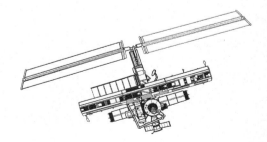

# WOULD YOU RATHER...

Eat a waffle covered in mayonnaise
or
a pancake soaked in pickle juice?

Mountain cottage with no internet
or
city mansion with constant construction?

# WOULD YOU RATHER...

Have the ability to instantly
solve any math problem
or
understand the secrets
of the universe with advanced knowledge?

Only watch one single movie
for the rest of your life
or
only eat the same food
for the rest of your life?

# WOULD YOU RATHER...

Have super weird dreams forever
or
never dream again?

Have six months of winter
or
six months of summer?

# WOULD YOU RATHER...

Ride a piggy
or
give a piggyback ride?

Have a Giraffe neck
or
Elephant's trunk?

# WOULD YOU RATHER...

Have to publicly speak every day
or
get a visible tattoo you really hated?

swim with eels
or
sleep in a bat-filled cave?

# WOULD YOU RATHER...

Be locked overnight
in an amusement park
or
in a shopping mall?

Have only cake
or
only pie as your
forever-birthday dessert?

# WOULD YOU RATHER...

Be unable to remember names
or
unable to remember faces?

Be overdressed
or
underdressed in a party?

# WOULD YOU RATHER...

Spend a month backpacking around Norway or around Japan?

Have an apartment in Paris or Barcelona?

# WOULD YOU RATHER...

Have a fluffy squirrel tail
or
have huge elephant ears?

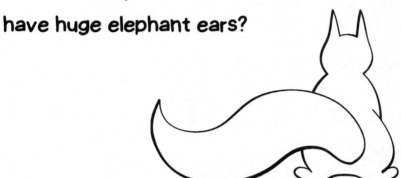

Be the best dancer in the school
or
Best singer?

# WOULD YOU RATHER...

Smell like a chocolate
or
vanilla?

Earn money
mowing laws
or
Running a snow cone stand?

# WOULD YOU RATHER...

Swim in slime
or
swim in muddy water?

Figure out Rubik's Cube
or
code a website?

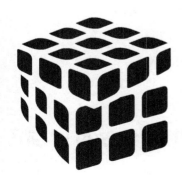

# WOULD YOU RATHER...

See a firework display or go to a concert?

Go skydiving or bungee jumping?

Sound like a sheep or a chicken when you laugh?

# WOULD YOU RATHER...

Have an extra finger
or
an extra toe?

Have a cactus for a blanket
or
rock for a pillow?

Live without the internet for a year
or
without electricity for a year?

# WOULD YOU RATHER...

Be bitten by a shark once
or
stung by a jelly fish 5 times?

Live where it is always warm and sunny
or
always cold and snowy?

# WOULD YOU RATHER...

Win 5 million cash tomorrow

or

100 million in 20 years time?

Have tons of money and no free time

or

have tons of free time and very little money?

# WOULD YOU RATHER...

Burst into spontaneous dance whenever you hear a song in public

or

wear an animal costume to school/work for a day?

have a fairy godmother

or

a genie lamp?

# WOULD YOU RATHER...

Skip instead of walking for a day
or
speak in rhymes while running errands?

Be able to speak every language fluently
or
have perfect navigation skills and never get lost?

# WOULD YOU RATHER...

Play with 10 puppies or 10 kittens?

Be a coder or a youtuber?

Be super smart or super lucky?

# WOULD YOU RATHER...

Perform a silly talent show in a park
or
wear a superhero cape and
help people with chores?

Experience the Northern Lights in Iceland
or
watch a sunset over the Sahara Desert?

# WOULD YOU RATHER...

Visit space or the animals of Madagascar?

Do the cooking or the cleaning?

Live in an amusement park or a zoo?

# WOULD YOU RATHER...

Go on a safari in Africa and see
elephants and lions
or
explore the Amazon rainforest
and encounter monkeys and toucans?

Jump in a trampoline park
or
skate at a skating rink?

# WOULD YOU RATHER...

Celebrate your birthday every single day

or

the same holiday every day?

Volunteer at an animal shelter

or

plant trees to help the environment?

# WOULD YOU RATHER...

Spend a week camping in the wilderness
or
a week exploring ancient ruins
in a far-off land?

Have a movie night every Friday
or
a game night every Saturday?

# WOULD YOU RATHER...

Have five good friends
or
one best friend?

Live in a world with magical creatures
like dragons and unicorns or
in a world with alien civilizations?

# WOULD YOU RATHER...

Play a board game or a card game?

Be a prince (Boy) / princess (Girl)
or
a Superman (Boy)/ Superwoman (Girl)?

# WOULD YOU RATHER...

Have a picnic in the park with your family
or
go on an adventurous hike in the mountains?

Eat dog food or cat food?

# WOULD YOU RATHER...

Live alone in a giant house
or
live in a regular-sized house with
100 roommates?

Never have a pet again
or
never have a TV again?

# WOULD YOU RATHER...

Live in a science museum or an art museum?

Travel the world or explore space?

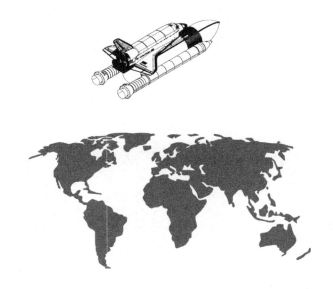

# WOULD YOU RATHER...

Build a snowman or have a snowball fight?

Be trapped in a video game or a board game?

Swim with dolphins or soar on an eagle's back?

# WOULD YOU RATHER...

Pet a polar bear or an arctic fox?

Be a fast runner or the highest jumper?

# WOULD YOU RATHER...

Play at the sand pit
or
paddle pool?

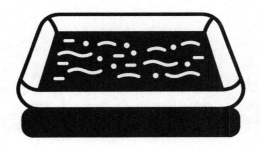

be able to control time
or
control the weather?

# WOULD YOU RATHER...

Not ever have to go to school
or
never have to do chores
for the rest of your life?

Play soccer with a beach ball
or
basketball with a watermelon?

# WOULD YOU RATHER...

Live in a treehouse or a castle?

Go on a rollercoaster or go skydiving?

Go snow skiing or water skiing?

# WOULD YOU RATHER...

Compete in a marathon wearing flippers
or
a swimming race with ski boots on?

Eat a cupcake
or
a slice of cake?

# WOULD YOU RATHER...

A nose the size of Pinocchio's
or
ears as large as Dumbo's?

Attend a formal dinner party
as a vampire or a werewolf?

# WOULD YOU RATHER...

Debate that cheese is the best topping,
even on ice cream,

or

argue that socks should be worn
on the hands instead of gloves?

Play tennis with water balloon balls

or

swim with inflatable arm floaties?

# WOULD YOU RATHER...

Tell spooky stories around the campfire
or
stargaze with a telescope all night?

Never have a life without air conditioning
or
never be able to use deodorant?

# WOULD YOU RATHER...

Have to shave your head

or

to have your nose pierced?

have to make a one-minute speech
in front of 10,000 people

or

have to kiss a frog?

# WOULD YOU RATHER...

Navigate the dark woods using
a glow-in-the-dark map
or
a trail of glow-in-the-dark socks?

Be chased by a herd of squirrels
or
have them challenge you to
a game of acorn-fetch?

# WOULD YOU RATHER...

Encounter a lost hiker who needs your help finding their way back

or

stumble upon a wounded animal that needs your assistance?

Watch a movie where all the characters are played by geese

or

a play where all the actors are dressed as giant vegetables?

# WOULD YOU RATHER...

Eat sushi or burgers?

Take a friend on your family vacation
or
join your friend on their family vacation?

# WOULD YOU RATHER...

Debate the Earth is flat
or
argue that vegetables plot
against humans through telepathy?

Sit next to someone who narrates the movie
or
comments on actors' fashion during a play?

# WOULD YOU RATHER...

only be able to eat healthy foods

or

only eat junk food?

Have the power to make objects appear out of thin air

or

be able to teleport anywhere?

# WOULD YOU RATHER...

Lose on television
or
win with nobody watching?

Live in a house by the ocean
or
in a cabin in the mountains?

# WOULD YOU RATHER...

A magical map that shows you
all the hidden treasures
or
a passport that lets you travel to
any country without needing a visa?

Be the school quarterback
or
have the lead role in the school musical?

# WOULD YOU RATHER...

Explore the Amazon Rainforest
or
climb to the top of Mount Everest?

Be tall and slow or short and fast?

Have to play a match on
New Year's Day or Thanksgiving?

# WOULD YOU RATHER...

Be a member of the Avengers
or
the Justice League?

Babysit a baby Godzilla
or
teach a baby T-Rex to play fetch?

# WOULD YOU RATHER...

Search for hidden treasures
in a haunted house
or
on a deserted island full of
talking monkeys?

Be captain of a sports team
or
President of the Drama Club?

# WOULD YOU RATHER...

Own a coffee shop or a bakery?

Own a mansion or a private jet?

# WOULD YOU RATHER...

Be a famous songwriter or a famous drummer?

Be your family dog or a wild wolf?

# WOULD YOU RATHER...

Would you rather burp
or
fart all of the time?

Be chased by stinky cheese monsters
or
a gang of slime-covered mutant snails?

# WOULD YOU RATHER...

Have one huge eye
or
three small eyes?

Have bubble gum stuck
in your hair
or
step your barefoot
into a doggie doo?

# WOULD YOU RATHER...

Eat spaghetti with chocolate sauce
or
ice cream with ketchup?

Let a spider climb over you
or
let a snake slither across you?

# WOULD YOU RATHER...

Lick a dirty trash
or
bathroom floor?

Wear underwear made of slimy jelly
or
socks filled with squishy pudding?

# WOULD YOU RATHER...

To never use shampoo again
or
go without toothpaste for life?

Smell like rotten eggs or sour milk all the time?

# CONGRATULATIONS!

Now that you've come this far, here's your.....

# CHOOSE THE RIGHT SHADOW.

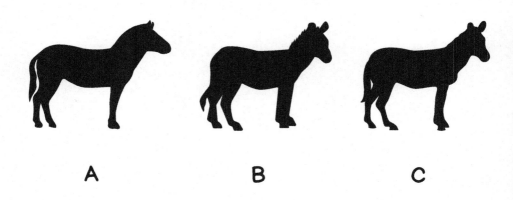

A  B  C

# PICK THE ODD ONE OUT.

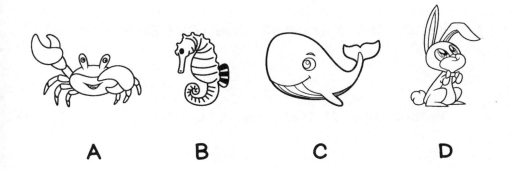

A          B          C          D

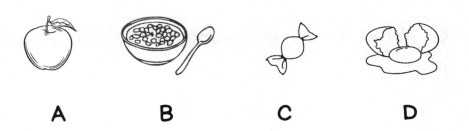

A          B          C          D

# RIDDLES TO RACK YOUR BRAIN!

1. What has one head, one foot and four legs?

2. What kind of tree can you hold in your hand?

3. You buy me to eat, but I am never eaten. What am I?

4. What did the mushroom say to the fungus?

# BONUS ANSWERS

Choose the right shadow.

B


Pick the odd one out.

D

C


Riddles to quack your brain

1. Bed
2. Palm tree
3. A plate
4. You are a fun-guy.

# If you like what we do,
# Leave us a review.

★★★★★

*Your support means a lot to our small business.*

# PHOE SPRINTS

Printed in Great Britain
by Amazon